Do Vo...   ...eally

Raintree is an imprint of Capstone Global Library Limited, a company incorporated in England and Wales having its registered office at 264 Banbury Road, Oxford, OX2 7DY – Registered company number: 6695582

www.raintree.co.uk
myorders@raintree.co.uk

Text © Capstone Global Library Limited 2022
The moral rights of the proprietor have been asserted.

Edited by Megan Peterson
Designed by Ted Williams
Original illustrations © Capstone Global Library Limited 2022
Picture research by Jo Miller
Production by Spencer Rosio
Originated by Capstone Global Library Ltd
Printed and bound in India

978 1 3982 1558 0 (hardback)
978 1 3982 1566 5 (paperback)

British Library Cataloguing in Publication Data
A full catalogue record for this book is available from the British Library.

Acknowledgements
We would like to thank the following for permission to reproduce photographs: agefotostock: Adrian Warren/ardea.com, 11, 15; Getty Images: Johner Images, 10; iStockphoto: through-my-lens, 7; Minden Pictures: Barry Mansell, 5; National Geographic Image Collection: Bruce Dale, 17; Newscom: Haroldo Palo Jr/NHPA/Photoshot, cover; Shutterstock: belizar, 13, 16, Bepoh624, design elelment, DreamLoud, 20, Mendesbio, 9, 19, owatta, design elelment

Every effort has been made to contact copyright holders of material reproduced in this book. Any omissions will be rectified in subsequent printings if notice is given to the publisher.

Contents

Words in **bold** are in the glossary.

Hungry bats

It is night-time. Most of the world is fast asleep. Vampire bats are just waking up. They have been sleeping all day. Now they need food. Do these bats eat fruit and vegetables? How about insects? No! Vampire bats want to drink blood.

Meet the bats

Earth is home to more than 1,200 types of bats. Bats might look like birds. But they are **mammals**. Bats are the only mammals that can fly.

Vampire bats are a special type of bat. They eat and drink only blood. They don't eat anything else! They get all the **nutrients** they need from blood.

Vampire bats are **nocturnal**. They sleep during the day. They hang upside down from the roofs of caves. They can easily drop down and fly away. Vampire bats sleep in **colonies** of hundreds of bats. They huddle together to stay warm.

Party all night

At night, vampire bats hunt for food. They fly with two wings. Bats have long arms and fingers. Skin covers these arms and fingers to make wings.

fingers

fingers

A vampire bat's **wingspan** is up to 38 centimetres (15 inches). The bat's thumbs stick out from its wings. Bats use their thumbs to climb, walk and jump.

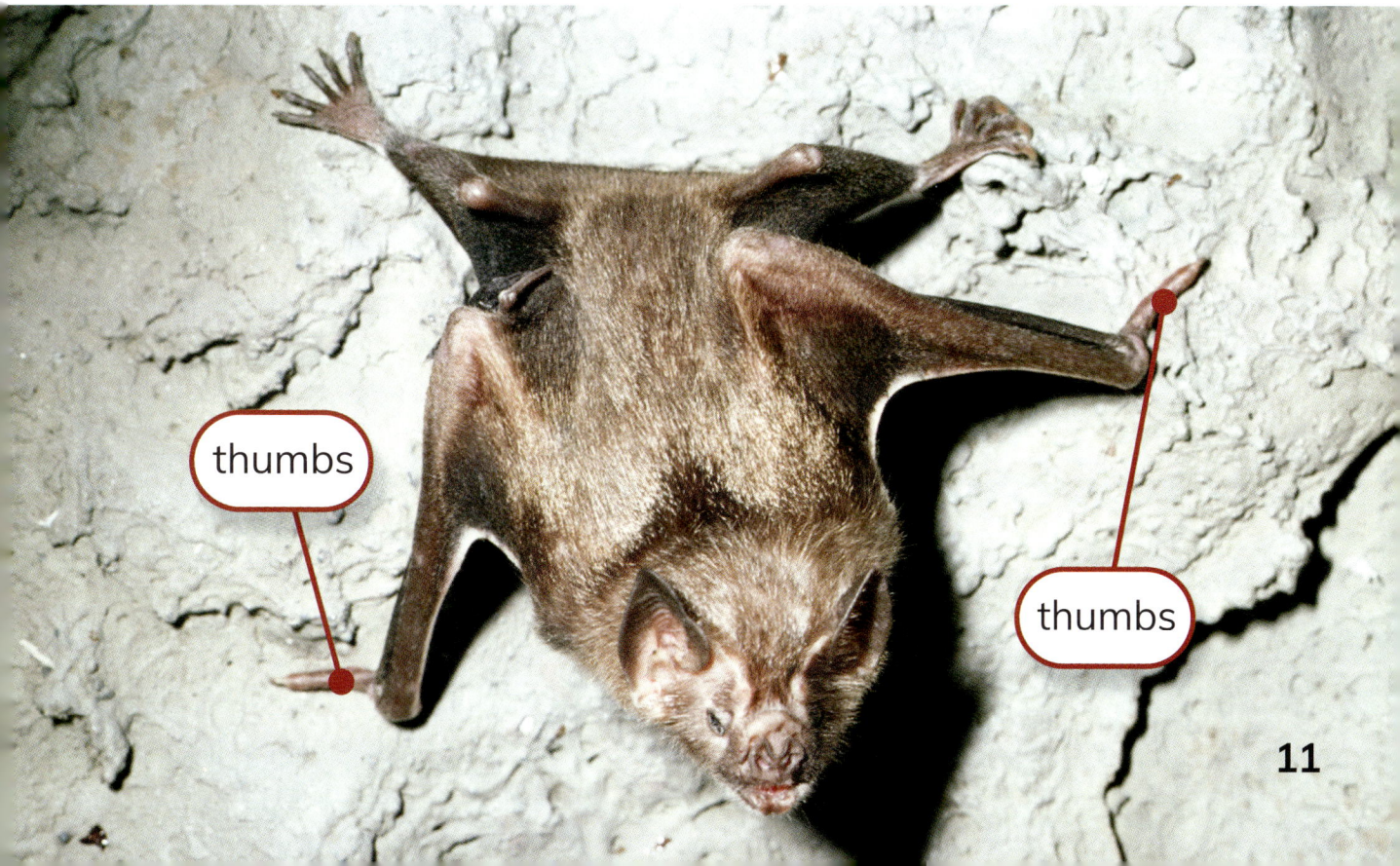

thumbs

thumbs

Echo! Echo!

Vampire bats can't see well in the dark. How do they find food? Bats make a high-**pitched** sound as they fly. This sound bounces off objects and returns to the bat. The vampire bat listens for the **echo**. Then the bat flies towards its meal.

Quiet, please

Vampire bats feed on the blood of cows, horses and pigs. Some drink bird blood.

Vampire bats are sneaky. They land quietly on the ground. Vampire bats leap onto sleeping animals. The bats' noses feel heat. They can find warm blood flowing near the skin's surface. Then it's time to eat.

Blood feast

Vampire bats bite with razor-sharp teeth. The sleeping animals don't feel the bite. They stay asleep. Blood spills out into a pool. The bats lap it up with their tongues. They eat for about 20 minutes.

Vampire bat bodies are only about 8 cm (3 inches) long. But they can hold a lot of blood. In one year, 100 bats can drink the blood of 25 cows!

Dangerous and helpful

Vampire bat bites are dangerous. These bats can carry diseases such as **rabies**. A vampire bat's bite can pass along the disease. The bite can make animals sick.

Vampire bats might be helpful! Their spit stops blood from **clotting**. The blood keeps flowing so the bat can eat. Doctors study bat spit. The spit could be used in medicine to help people.

Vampire bat greetings card

What you need:

- card
- colouring pens or crayons
- pencil

What to do:

1. Make a greetings card for your friend. Choose any colour card.

2. Fold the paper in half.

3. Using crayons or pens, decorate the front of the card. How do you think a vampire bat would decorate it?

4. Inside the card, write a note to your friend. Sign your card with your pretend vampire bat name. Then give the card to your friend!

Glossary

clot become thicker and more solid; blood clots to stop the body from bleeding

colony large group of animals that lives together

echo sound that returns after a travelling sound hits an object

mammal warm-blooded animal that breathes air and has hair or fur; female mammals feed milk to their young

nocturnal active at night and resting during the day

nutrient something that is needed to stay healthy and strong

pitch highness or lowness of a sound

rabies deadly disease that people and animals can get from the bite of an infected animal

wingspan distance between the tips of a pair of wings when fully open

Find out more

Books

The Bat Book, Charlotte Milner (DK Children, 2020)

Bloodsuckers of the Animal World (Disgusting Creature Diets), Jody Sullivan Rake (Raintree, 2016)

Vampire Bats (Mammals in the Wild), Kathryn Clay (Raintree, 2020)

Websites

www.bbc.co.uk/bitesize/topics/z6882hv
Learn more about animals, from mammals to minibeasts.

www.dkfindout.com/uk/animals-and-nature/animal-kingdom
Find out more about the animal kingdom.

Index